*"The biggest communication problem is we do not listen to understand. We listen to reply."*

# PODCASTING PRO
# BASICS

## ORLANDO RIOS

# Podcasting Pro
# BASICS

ISBN-13: 978-0692640975
ISBN-10: 0692640975

Podcasting Pro
www.podcastingpro.com
info@podcastingpro.com

Printed in U.S.A

# Contents

# Introduction

The world of podcasting has become a major player in the realm of digestible media. In fact, at the time of this writing almost one in three Americans has listened to a podcast at one point in their life. What once seemed to be just a novel idea, the podcast is now a highly lucrative platform that is a direct competitor to the radio industry. In 2015, there were over three billion downloads!

The best part about the podcast is that anyone can do it. You don't need a special license, you don't need a degree, and you don't need a big bank account to have your own show. With an idea and little commitment, everyone has the ability to share their thoughts and art with the entire world. And if you develop a good audience, you even have the ability to make a good living with sponsorships!

For those who want to start their own show, the idea can be a little intimidating. What equipment is best? How do I sound like a professional? How do I get my show on iTunes? These are all questions you most likely have. The good news is that it's relatively easy to get started. With a little direction and a little practice, you can be podcasting in as little as a week.

In *Podcasting Pro Basics*, I will help you get going as quickly and economically responsible as possible. With over 300 hours of podcasting experience and as a producer of some of the top shows on iTunes, I've developed a wealth of information on the subject that I can't wait to share.

You will learn which equipment is best for podcasting at any budget, which software is ideal for recording, some tips on developing your show and even some of the editing techniques I use to get my shows sounding crisp and enjoyable. Then, to top it all off, we will get your show published on iTunes and Stitcher—the top two podcast listening platforms in the world.

Let's get started!

# Chapter 1
# Getting Started

If you are the creative entrepreneurial type, you may be tempted to move extremely fast in getting your podcast going. You may already be thinking about sponsors, the compliments you're going to get on your show, and how you're going to be sharing a spot on the charts with Joe Rogan.

It's great to have that drive. It will ultimately lead you to success, but there are a few things you should ask yourself and figure out before you jump in too deep. As you get started you want to have a plan and be able to follow through. You want to make sure the financial investment you're making isn't going to leave you with wasted dollars that you could've spent elsewhere. The show has to be well thought out and good from the beginning. Think of how many television pilots get canned because the subject matter or quality of the show isn't up to par. You have one chance to make an impression, so you may as well go in prepared.

# Investment

There is going to be some financial investment on your part in some way if you want to get serious about podcasting. Chances are that, if you're reading this book, you at least plan to make a serious effort. This is good, but we need to be honest with ourselves.

We all know the type of people who decide one day they are going to take up the guitar and go out and buy a Les Paul before learning an E chord. Don't be that person. On the contrary, you also don't want to go waste money on a cheap guitar that you will despise in a month.

The key is finding a happy median.

It's no secret that equipment is going to be your biggest investment in this venture. At this point in your podcasting career, hosting will cost you almost nothing and marketing through social media is mostly free. There are some other marketing investments you may want to make, but I'm going to recommend you put your money in the equipment to start.

On the next page are some examples of starting packages (assuming you already have a decent computer) and what they would cost as of the writing of this book. You will notice a huge difference between better and best. Remember how I talked about the musician buying the Les Paul before he knew an E chord? The best is the Les Paul. You should only go best if you are a seasoned vet, have millions of downloads a year or are already a rich mega-celebrity, but I thought I'd include it anyway to show how crazy things can get.

**Good $150**

- Quality Multi-Directional USB Microphone
- Free Recording Software
- 250MB Monthly Hosting (+$15/Month)

Best if your show will be no more than an hour once a week and mostly be solo or with one other guest.

**Better $400**

- Three Dynamic Microphones
- Three Cables
- Three Table Stands
- USB Mixer
- Free Recording Software
- 400MB Monthly Hosting (+$20/Month)
- Pro Editing Software Subscription (+$15/month)

Best if your show will be an hour or more, once a week or more and will consistently have more than two guests.

**Best $2000**

- Four Top of the Line Cardioid Dynamic Microphones
- Four Cables
- Four Table Stands

As you can see from the pricing, you can get started for a very reasonable price that won't make a dent in your finances or you can blow your savings and possibly never see a return.

I would personally stand by all of these options to give you a quality outcome, even the "Good" package. The key, as I've mentioned, is to be honest with yourself, where you are and where you're going. Most people start their podcasts as a solo show with maybe one other guest at a time. The "Good" package is more than sufficient for that.

You will notice that the hosting prices are a little extra. In reality, you can get started for as little as $5 a month. It just depends on how long and how many podcasts you will do a month. Platforms like iTunes & Stitcher don't charge to give access to your show, but you need the hosting to be able to feed it to them.

Some packages also include a Pro Editing Software Subscription. Obviously there are some you can just buy, but the one that I use has a small subscription fee. What the advanced software gives you is the ability to clean up the audio, mix other files in, and mix it down to a good quality MP3 at the best file size possible. If you're on a Mac you're in luck because you probably have Garage Band, which will probably do the trick for you.

Any way you decide to go, make sure you're comfortable with it. When we get to the equipment chapter, I will list a variety of options all of which are in use by some of the most popular shows on iTunes & Stitcher. The content is what's most important of course, but the content has to be digestible in a pleasant way to the human ear.

## Format

If you want to build a real audience, it's a good idea to get a format for your show locked down. Think of your favorite television or radio shows. You know when new episodes are going to be available, you know the time commitment that's going to be involved and you know generally what the basis of each show is going to be.

It takes a big commitment for a listener to decide to listen to your show once and a near marriage for them to subscribe and listen to it regularly.

### Categories

The first thing you will need to decide is what category your show is going to be in. Will you be covering topics in the news? Maybe you're strictly a health & fitness show. Maybe you have the gift of comedy. Whatever the basis of your show is, you will need to pick a category and try to stick with it in the beginning. You can always change it later if your show morphs into something else, but for all things good, pick one. It helps people find you, gives you a better chance at becoming ranked, and helps keep things consistent.

## Time

It's a good idea to figure out what length of time you want each show to be beforehand. Sometimes conversations can run with quality content, but you need to be aware always where you are with your show. Remember, the easier you make it for the listener to predict their time commitment to your show the more likely they will listen.

I've heard shows that are a quick 15 minutes and I've heard shows that are over three hours long. There is no right answer to the amount of time each episode should be, but you should try to be consistent with each episode.

## Schedule

One of the biggest keys to getting ranked and keep listeners is having a dedicated schedule. In the iTunes charts, I've seen first-hand what releasing episodes on a certain day at a certain time consistently can do. Plain and simple; if you're getting more plays in a certain period of time than anyone else, no matter what episode it is, you will climb in the ranks.

If you were a podcast listener and knew that every Monday at nine in the morning a new episode of your favorite podcast was going to be available, you could always look forward to it. Alternatively, if you hadn't listened to Monday's podcast you would know that you have all week to listen to it before the next one releases so you don't fall behind.

By following this philosophy and setting a consistent release schedule, you will be doing your rankings and your listeners a huge favor.

# Chapter 2
# Equipment and Software

As we mentioned in the investment section of this book, equipment is going to be the biggest expense for you to get started. But remember what I said earlier. Don't be the person who buys the Les Paul before knowing how to play a chord unless you already have a substantial following or are a celebrity. So be smart and honest with yourself when selecting your equipment.

Following on from that thought, it's not necessarily bad to plan for growth. The worst times I've ever come across as a podcast producer were when I wasn't prepared for a certain amount of guests, meaning I didn't have enough equipment or equipment that was versatile enough to handle the curveballs.

## Microphones

The most important part of the podcast is the discussion. The microphone is responsible for capturing that discussion in the clearest way. Here is where you will find your biggest improvement from something like the mic in your laptop. If you had to allocate budget for your setup, this is where I'd put the bulk of it. We'll get a little into the science of each type of microphone, then I'll list my suggestions.

## Types

There are two types of microphones we would use for podcasting: Dynamic and Condenser. In almost all live sound setups people use Dynamic style mics. They are relatively inexpensive and are usually really sturdy units. You may have seen these used at a live show by your favorite band or comedian. They are also used to mic guitar amps in the studio. The most popular one of all time is the Shure SM-58. The only drawback to a Dynamic mic is that it will most likely need a preamp of some sort as it doesn't take phantom power. Luckily, if you are going to use one of the non-usb Dynamic mics I list, you will need a board anyway—which usually has a decent enough gain.

Condenser microphones are usually used in studios for vocals and stringed, non-amplified instruments. They have a much greater frequency response and are much more sensitive than a dynamic mic. These will no doubt have to be plugged into a soundboard. Condensers require phantom power to be used.

Between the two types, I'd personally recommend a Dynamic microphone. While Condensers can pick up your voice beautifully, they will also pick up all the dead air and any little noise around you. Dynamics will, in most scenarios, only pick up the voice directly in front of them, resulting in a clear tone without the background noise. This will save you a lot of time in the editing process if you don't have a super soundproof studio.

## Directionality

Microphones have one of three directionalities. The directionality of a microphone indicates which direction the microphone best picks up sound. The types are unidirectional, bidirectional, and omnidirectional.

The most commonly used is the unidirectional, like a Shure SM-58. These are also known as cardioids. These microphones take sound in from the front only, which is perfect in a podcast setting with one or more people if everyone has their own mic. This is the ideal choice.

Next is the bidirectional microphone. You can probably guess that bi-directional means two ways. To clarify that, a bidirectional microphone will pick up audio from the front and rear. If you didn't have more than one microphone and had one other guest, this would be the choice. You would be face to face and have this directionality of a microphone in between.

Finally, we have the omnidirectional microphone. This microphone has no directionality, meaning that it will pick up from all directions. These are mostly used in live setups for choirs. If you were in a situation where you had one mic or not enough mics for each guest, you would choose this directionality of a microphone. You would stick this in the middle of the table and everyone would huddle around it. Because of its vast range, you would not get as clear and upfront voice from everyone, but it could definitely help you out and still give you a decent product post-editing.

**Recommendations**

To simplify this I am only going to list three different microphones. While there are many more out there, these are the ones that I can vouch for and that most of the top podcasters use. Since the amount of guests you plan to have, if any, is such an important factor I will also make a note of that. The prices will range from good to top of the line. Most of us won't use the top of the line. I don't even. But I thought I'd list it in case you're already big, have the pocketbook and are in for the long haul.

**Blue Yeti**

**The Blue Yeti**

This will be the only USB microphone I'm going to recommend. The benefit of a USB microphone is that you won't have to get a board. It will have its own gain and will work with nearly every program on your computer that would ever need a microphone. The only con to the USB microphone is that you will be limited by the amount of USB ports and ram you have if you plan to have more than one.

The Blue Yeti not only looks super cool, it also is an extremely good quality microphone for the price. It is also very versatile. It offers a switch for every single directionality you could want. You heard that right. This microphone is a cardioid, bidirectional, omnidirectional, and even a stereo mic.

If you plan to podcast by yourself, plan to ever have one other in-person guest, and want to save a ton of money, this is the microphone to get.

**Price:** Around $100 (Price Varies Based On Color)
**Type:** Both Dynamic and Condenser
**Directionality:** Cardioid, Bidirectional, Omnidirectional + Stereo
**Hidden Costs:** Will Need Windscreen
**Where To Buy:** Amazon

**GLS Audio ES-58**

I'm sure you've heard me mention the Shure SM58 a couple of times by now. There is no doubt the 58 is the most popular microphone in the world. But I have a tip for you. There's a company called GLS that makes a perfect replica of the Shure SM58 at half the price. Usually I would never recommend what would be considered a knock-off, but this microphone is legit. I've bought several over the years that have lasted me to this day. I've abused the hell out of them and they still sound amazing.

This is strictly a cardioid microphone and will need a board with an XLR input to use. It will also need a pre-amp or gain, which most boards or XLR input devices will have.

If you plan to have more than one in-person guest consistently, and want everyone to have their own microphone with a crisp sound, this is the way to go if you don't have the big bucks. These microphones are incredibly cheap, but you will need a proper board for those XLR inputs with gain. A setup with these microphones allows for the most expansion for in-person guests.

**Price:** $30
**Type:** Dynamic
**Directionality:** Cardioid
**Hidden Costs:** Will Need Mic Stand, XLR Cable and Windscreen
**Where To Buy:** Amazon

**Shure SM7B**

This is the king of podcasting microphones. Hell, this is the king of radio microphones too. When it comes to extremely professional recording of any type of talk show, a Shure SM7B is what will be used.

Strictly a cardioid microphone, the Shure SM7B has a flat wide-range frequency response that has the cleanest and most natural reproduction of sound. It also has great protection from the hum of electronic devices. For the cleanest, clearest, crispest sound this THE mic. As with the GLS ES-58, you will need a board with an XLR input that has a pre-amp or gain.

The only drawback to this microphone is the price. If it's just you, it's going to be expensive. If you have guests, I hope you have a good credit limit. The good news is that I don't feel there is anywhere up in quality to go from here. This is it.

I will note that, as the host, you should always sound the best. It's okay to treat yourself to this microphone and give the GLS ES-58s to your guests. They can all go in the same board.

**Price:** $350
**Type:** Dynamic
**Directionality:** Cardioid
**Hidden Costs:** Will Need Mic Stand and XLR Cable
**Where To Buy:** Amazon

**Shure SM7B**

# Boards

If you're not going with a USB microphone, you are going to need some sort of XLR input with gain. This is where the mixing board comes in. There are more benefits to a mixing board than just the inputs. A mixing board allows you to set the levels of each microphone individually.

With multiple guests, there is no doubt someone may have a deeper or louder voice than somebody else. Having the ability to set the levels for each microphone in this situation will give your podcast a balanced volume. This is beautiful to the listeners' ears. There is nothing worse than having to constantly adjust your volume as a listener.

There are only a couple of things to make sure of when shopping for a new mixing board. Number one, you want to make sure the board is a USB board. This is how you will get your audio into your computer for recording. Second, you need to make sure the board has a good gain or pre-amp. If you are following my recommendations, you will be using a Dynamic microphone and a good gain or pre-amp will be essential. Lastly, you will need to decide how many XLR inputs you need. Any more than five inputs is probably pushing what you will ever need.

**Mackie ProFX8v2 8-Channel Mixer**

The Mackie brand, in my opinion, has the best pre-amps in its mixing boards. It's the brand I personally use. They also within the last year have improved their USB models immensely. All things we like to hear when we think of pairing a Dynamic Cardioid with it for podcasting. This particular model will give you everything you need and four XLR inputs. There will hardly ever be a moment when you will have more than three guests, so this should be more than sufficient. If you want to plan for even more guests, they also have boards in this series that go all the way up to 22 XLR inputs. But that's a little ridiculous.

**Price: $230**
**XLR Inputs: Four**
**Where To Buy: Amazon**

Mackie ProFX8v2 8-Channel Mixer

### Behringer XENYX X1204USB Premium Mixer

If you can't shell out the extra bill for a mixer, your next best bet is this mixer. This is the mixer that I've done well over 100 hours on. It's reliable and will get the job done. My only knock on this particular brand is that I don't think the gain is as good as the Mackies. With all that said, it is not going to make or break you to choose this or the Mackie. But if you're already going with the Shure SM7B microphone, you sure as hell better be getting the Mackie.

**Price:** $150
**XLR Inputs:** Four
**Where To Buy:** Amazon

## Recording Software

This is probably going to be the easiest decision for you to make because I'm only going to give you one option. When choosing recording software, the goal is something that will take that USB signal and capture it accurately and reliably. You would think I was going to recommend something that was extremely expensive. Actually, what I'm going to recommend is absolutely free, no strings attached. It's called Audacity and I've been using it for every podcast I've done or will do till the end of time. There really just isn't anything better for what we are trying to accomplish. It's also extremely simple and frills-free to use. Plus, it's free.

**Audacity**
**Price: Free**
**OS: Mac and PC**
**Where To Download: AudacityTeam.org**

## Editing Software

Once we've got a good recording done, we're going to need to edit the track. We're going to want to trim it, reduce noise, and set peak levels. If we have an opening theme song or commercials we need to work in, we will have to mix those tracks in. This is where the editing software comes in.

While Audacity has the ability to mix and trim tracks, it does lack the ability to do the polishing that will make our finished episode sound great to a listener. There are tons of applications for editing audio and I've only tried a handful of them, so you may be able to find something suitable on your own. The main plugin to look for in a program is the ability to hard limit and reduce noise. There's no doubt heavyweights like Logic Pro and Pro Tools will do the job and then some, but those programs are expensive. If you happen to already have those programs, you're set. If not, here are a couple of less expensive programs that have the plugins to make your podcast shine. Again, there may be other options for you out there. These are only a couple I personally have tried or know are being used in the industry.

## Garage Band

If you have a Mac, you more than likely to already have Garage Band. It's the younger, less experienced brother of the $199 Logic Pro. Luckily for you, it has just enough power to mix and polish your podcast episode. I personally do not use Garage Band to edit my podcasts, but I know plenty of major people who do. Plus it will cost you nothing if you have a Mac.

**Price: Free**
**OS: Mac**

## Adobe Audition

I have the big boy Logic Pro, but when it comes to editing podcasts I actually prefer to use Adobe Audition. Every single polishing element we should use exists and works absolutely great. The design isn't confusing, every plugin is easy to find, and it exports a perfect product. Back in the day you used to have to buy this software for a big fee, but with Adobe's new subscription model you can have it for a monthly fee. If you're putting out a bunch of podcast episodes, it is worth it.

**Price: $19.99/Month**
**OS: Mac and PC**
**Download: Amazon or Adobe**

# Chapter 3
# Pre-Show Prep

Now that you've got all of your equipment in order, the next step in your podcasting journey is to produce your first show. But what you will learn from your first show and every show that follows it is that there is a bit of anxiety that goes into the setup. So many things can go wrong. I've seen others do it a thousand times. In fact, I've even seen myself do it a handful of times. You can get through an entire show and a mic wasn't on or, even worse, you forgot to press the record button. Maybe the mic placement was so off it is impossible to have a balanced output. Whatever that disaster may be, it can be avoided with proper planning.

## Show Outline

Before you get to setting up your equipment for the show, it's a good idea to put together a conversational outline of the show you are about to record. This helps keep the flow of your show and keeps it from bouncing around too many subjects, making the listener confused.

### Topics of Discussion

Now, when I say create a show outline, I don't mean to use it as a strict script of what to say and when to say it. Podcasts should still feel free flowing, but it's good to have a roadmap to make sure you still are going to point B. So, rather than a script, just jot down topics of discussion that you want to talk about on your show. I would recommend having about ten topics, and in a good order that goes with the flow of conversation.

**Background Checks & Emergency Topics**

If you are interviewing somebody, it's also good practice to do a little background check before the show. Learn some interesting things to talk about and have them on your outline as backup questions. I say this because sometimes guests themselves can be the reason a show flops. Normally, when you ask a guest a question or bring up a topic, you would hope they would answer or discuss the topic and expand on it. Unfortunately, every once in a while you will get the guest who gives you the one to two word answer leaving you scrambling to move on. When that happens, look to your outline and what I call emergency topics.

**Watch the Time**

In this same regard, pay attention to time. You don't want to go to short and you don't want to go too long. Set what you consider to be a short podcast and decide what is too long. From my experience, the sweet spot in podcasts is about 45 minutes to an hour. Of course, if you're a mega star like Joe Rogan, you can go for three hours. But that's for the hardcore listener.

With an outline and basis of time set, you will set yourself up for the best possible outcome. I will remind you, though, to have fun. Don't be so stringent on your outline. Just like Google, it's there to guide and save you when you need it.

# Mic Placement

If you are taking my recommendation of using a Dynamic cardioid microphone, placement is going to be of the utmost importance. The way the mic is designed, the top will have to be pointed towards yours and any of your guests' mouths.

## Distance

Now, nobody should have their mouth directly on the microphone. You want to keep a distance of about six inches to a foot. Any closer and you are guaranteed to get clipping of the signal. Any further and you're sure to pick up a lot of dead air.

## Pops

Another issue with mic placement is pops. A pop is a rush of air that comes from the mic and creates that 'poof' sound that is so annoying to the listener. I'm sure you will have a windscreen on your mic that will help deaden this, but there is a little tip to help avoid this further. Slightly angle the microphone up so that the voice waves pass through and over instead of directly in. This will keep the majority of the voice captured and some of that extra noise passed over.

## Bangs

Depending on what kind of mic stands you use, I will warn you about another issue I've come across. If you have a guest who gets really animated when they talk, they will most likely tap the table or hit the table at some point. If you're using a table top mic stand and this happens, you're going to get loud bangs that echo through the stand and into the microphone. It sounds terrible. Tell yourself and your guests to avoid hitting the table at any cost. Also try to find a stand that has some kind of suspension system so that it can deaden those kinds of interferences. If all else fails and you have a table top stand, just get some kind of foam or sponge-like material to rest the stand on. It will go a long way.

# Setting Levels

Once we have our outline ready and our mic placement solid, it's time to plug everything in and set the levels. After we think we have the levels all set nicely, it will then be time for a test recording.

This is where your podcast will really shine. Before we can even think about going in and polishing later, we have to give ourselves a good quality product to begin with. As the saying goes, you can't polish a turd.

## Levels

Depending on whether you are using a USB mic or coming through a board, you will have to check and monitor a couple of different things. If you're using a USB, you're mainly going to be looking at your recording program (like Audacity) to see how hot the signal is coming in. If you're using a series of microphones through a board, you will have to monitor each individual microphone on the board and then also see what the full signal looks like in the recording program.

For the USB microphone, folks, you should have a gain switch on your microphone. Open up your recording program, select your microphone as the input and click record. Now talk at the volume you expect to talk at the distance from the microphone you plan to be. Look how the waves on the recording program behave. You will notice ticks or levels with numbers on them. The sweet spot is between -0.05 and 1. If you get a wave that fluctuates between those two points, you are solid. Adjust the gain of your mic accordingly if not. It's also pretty easy to know that if you see a red flash anywhere in a recording program, your volume is too hot. So if you see that somewhere else, lower that gain till it goes away.

For the mixing board people, we first need to go through each microphone into the board and set the levels there. If you have one of the boards I recommended, you should have a gain knob. More than likely, you're going to want this turned up pretty high if you are using a Dynamic cardioid microphone. I usually have mine at least at 75% so I can get the biggest signal. Talk into each microphone and monitor each microphone's individual level. Your board should have a track of lights and/or at least a red clip light. Get the signal of each microphone to the highest it can go without reaching that red point and give yourself a tick or two for extra padding. I'll also suggest, when you're testing each mic, press the mute button on the one's you aren't. This will help assure that each microphone is on and working, plus it will help you dial in that much further on the levels.

Once you have each microphone set on the mixing board at an optimal level, select the USB board in your recording program and do a test of the full output of the board. Just like the USB microphone setup, you should aim for that sweet spot of -0.05 and 1. Some boards' master output slider will allow you to increase the output to the USB; some won't. If you need more juice or less juice, just raise or lower all the individual microphone sliders accordingly.

In my experience, I think it's always best to give yourself something to work with. You can't fix an audio file that's too loud and clipping, but you can fix an audio file that's a little on the lower volume side in post-production. If you can get to the sweet spot that's amazing; if you're just under it it's okay. Just never, under any circumstance, be too hot. It's rarely fixable.

Now that you are all set up and you've tested everything, it's time for the fun part. Record your show! Remember to look at your outline when you need to, monitor the levels and adjust as needed. As soon as your show is complete, SAVE IMMEDIATELY. We then will take your creation to the editing phase, where we will make it all shine before publishing.

# Chapter 4
# Editing

With a great microphone and proper setup, editing can be a pretty easy part of the podcast production process. The goal of the editing phase is not to completely change what you recorded; rather, it's where we polish it up and make it pleasant for digestion. As I've mentioned several times in this book, we want to give the listener the most comfortable listening experience we can. We don't want them to think about having to adjust volume or any aspect other than listening to the show. Applying just a couple of techniques to the audio file can really make a difference and make it consistent across multiple devices.

The editing process is also an opportunity to add in other elements of the show. Maybe you have an opening theme to the show you would like to play. Perhaps you want to drop in some pre-recorded commercials. This would be the stage to do it in.

Assuming you recorded your podcast in Audacity, you will have to export the file if editing in another program. When you export the file I recommend doing so as a MONO Wave file.

Open your audio program, start a new session, and import your files. You will want to have a multitrack open if you plan to import extra files. Keep each section of the podcast on different tracks. If you have one, give the show intro its own track, the actual show its own track, and so on.

Now let's take our creation and make it shine. We will start with the actual show's editing process, take you through mixing in other files, and then finally exporting the final product.

# Trimming

The first step to editing your recorded show is to trim the audio. Most of the time you will have some dead air or pre-talk before the actual show starts. You will also, most likely, have the same at the end. To avoid this being published as part of your show it is important to trim out these parts.

Most of the time in your audio editing program you don't even have to listen to the sections you should delete. You will be able to look at the waves and see where you started and ended. Select the parts that don't belong on your show and delete. You don't need them anymore. Save.

This is the simplest part of the editing process.

# Hard Limiting

One of the biggest challenges of recording a podcast is dealing with peaks and lows. There is no doubt that during the show someone is going to get really excited and send the volume surging. Then, on the contrary, there is no doubt that someone is going to get really low when they talk.

We will aim to find a good balance of this by something we call hard limiting. When we hard limit, we boost the volume of the audio and 'limit' how far it can go. Now, with this process, you aren't deleting any of the signal. What is happening when you hard limit is its lowering the volume at places past your set limit. This keeps the audio from hitting the clip zone and creating heavy distortion.

Most audio programs have this plugin and it can go by many names. Some call it variable-gain audio level compression and some call it normalization. I do my editing in Adobe Audition, so for me it's called hard limiting. You can also find this in the free Audacity program I recommended for recording.

To understand how much boost and where to set the max amplitude, you have to look at the wave. When you see your waves, you will see where the majority and bulk of them are. Then you will see the big peaks that are abnormal, the majority of the file.

Our goal is to get the bulk of our wave as close to -0.01 as possible. Zoom in on the file and see how close the bulk of the wave is to that amount. Now look at the number ticks on the side and figure out what the difference is. This will be your boost amount in the hard limiter setting.

The next setting in the plugin would be the maximum amplitude amount. This should be -0.01. Select the entire wave and apply the plugin.

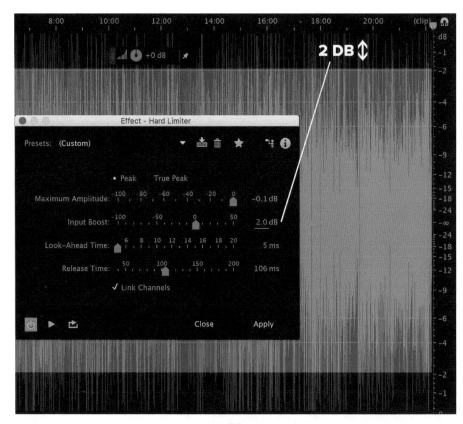

You should be left with a nice file with waves that stay within the -5 and -0.01 range. Give it a listen in both the low and high peak points and see how it sounds in your ears at a normal volume. If you need to, adjust, reduce or add boost accordingly. You're going to have peaks and valleys. Just make sure the bulk is within the range we talked about.

## Noise Reduction

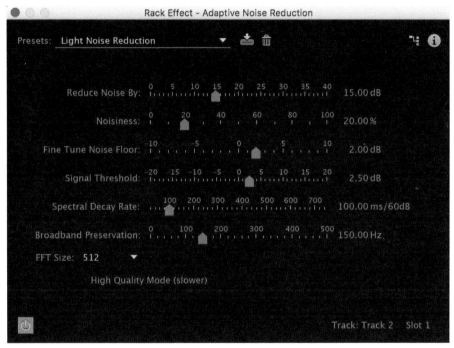

No matter what kind of mics we are using, it is inevitable that we will have some excess air in the recording. To keep the voices as upfront as possible we will do a process called Adaptive Noise Reduction. This plugin is available in Adobe Audition as well as the free Audacity program. In other programs this can sometimes also be called hiss reduction.

The first rule of thumb here is that you never want to overdo this process. If you go over it too much, it will really thin out the sound and make it tinny. So you want to use this process very conservatively.

In Adobe Audition, the Adaptive Noise Reduction has a setting called Light Noise Reduction. It's perfect. The reduction of noise is a maximum of 15%. This is just enough to take out that extra hiss while not affecting the mass of the actual sound. If you are in Audacity or another program, you will have to play with the settings a little bit and find your sweet spot the first time around. Just keep any reduction less than 15% or more and be super conservative. The goal is to lightly brush it up, not change the sound entirely.

## Mixing Tracks

Now that you've got your main file polished up you can mix in other elements of your podcast that you may want to include. As mentioned at the beginning of this chapter, you should keep all other imported audio on separate tracks.

There isn't much to this part of the process. You just want to make sure that the levels are equal to your main show's audio. Beware of any overlaps as they can really jump the audio level and cause a clip. If you need to overlap audio, fade in or fade out the ends into the other tracks. This will help keep the transition smooth and the amplitude from jumping.

Once you've checked the levels, made adjustments and are happy with your product, it is time to export it in a process called the mixdown.

## Final Mixdown

In Adobe Audition, this final process will be called a Multitrack Mixdown. In Audacity it will be called a Mix and Render. No matter what the terminology is, this process is about mixing everything we set up all together into one beautiful sounding file.

The most important part of this process is choosing the settings. While music sounds great in stereo, it is not the ideal format for podcasts. When you listen to music, 99% of the time in the stereo field the vocal is center in the mix and the instruments are spread out across the field. Since our priority here is vocal only, we don't need to have things spread across the field. This is why we will choose to have our mix MONO.

We will also want to choose the 192kb MP3 file format. When we are doing such a long audio file, we need to save it in a compressed format to save file size. MP3 allows us to maintain quality and our drive space. The bitrate is of debate, but if you're not including music there is no reason to do more than 192kb. By comparison, music you stream on Spotify is at 320kb but think about how many instruments that involves. Save the drive space since podcasts are generally vocal. The user wouldn't notice the difference anyway.

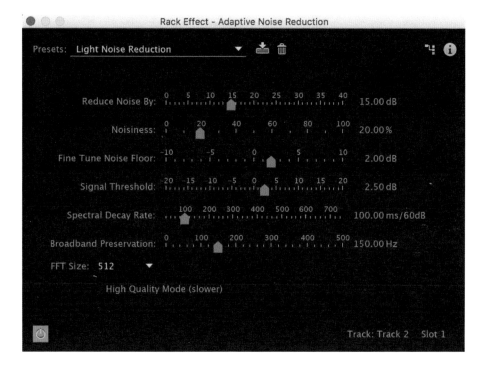

# Chapter 5
# Publishing

With a final product finally ready, it's time for us to move to the publishing stage. This is where we will get our show out to the world so, hopefully, millions will download and listen. While publishing seems like a complicated task, it's actually quite easy. If you've ever uploaded a file to the internet in your life, you already have the basic experience.

There is a bit of a setup to start, however. Luckily, once we're set we never have to really touch anything again unless we want to change the title, category or cosmetics of our show.

## Hosting

While you could just have MP3s available for download on your website, if you want to be on iTunes and Stitcher you will have to get a podcast hosting platform. The hosting platform will not only store all your files, but it will host your RSS feed. The RSS feed is what sends out all the data to the streaming services. I will make a big note here not to get ahead of yourself on the initial setup. You must have a host and at least one uploaded before you can submit to iTunes.

There are many podcast hosting platform options for you out there, but I am going to focus on the most popular service, Libsyn. This is the one most of the big players use and the one I recommend. Best of all, the pricing is great. Once you choose a hosting platform make sure you are ready to make the commitment. It's not easy to switch later on. If you do try to switch hosts, you will risk losing all the subscribers you built up. Not ideal.

**Libsyn**

The best part about Libsyn is the pricing. You can get started for as little as $5 a month. If you start growing, it's also really easy to upgrade. They submit to all the popular streaming services, give you your own page for you to share and stream, and at some levels of service even give you your own phone app!

When choosing your pricing plan, the main thing you want to consider is the monthly storage allowance. If your show is an hour and you follow my export recommendations, your show is going to be roughly 30mb. Calculate how many shows you plan to do a month and choose the appropriate plan for you.

The sign up is pretty self-explanatory, so I won't get too detailed on it here. The most important things to consider while filling out the initial information are the show slug, show category, title and description. While the category, title and description can change later, note that the show slug can't. So be sure to choose something you will stick with. This will help name your RSS feed and Libsyn show URL.

You will also be tasked with submitting the cover art for your show. This will be the image people see in iTunes that distinguishes your show. If you don't have design skills or a friend who does, I highly recommend **Fiverr.com**. You can get a great cover for under $100. This is your show's book cover. You can always change and update it later, but don't skimp on it.

**Uploading Your First Show**

Before we can submit to any of the streaming services, we need to upload our first show to Libsyn. Again, this is pretty straightforward. The only thing that I really want to point out here is the importance of your title and description. Podcasters use many different naming formats, but almost all of them number their episodes.

In the title, I suggest using the number of the show first then a brief, catchy title that easily portrays the subject matter of the episode. The description field is where you will really give the full synopsis on the episode.

For each episode, ignore the thumbnail image field. You don't need to upload an image for every episode. iTunes and Stitcher will just always use your show cover art and that's what you want.

When you publish you also have the option of setting the release date. Remember earlier in the book I mentioned it's good to have a dedicated schedule? This is where you can release the episode on any day or at any time you want.

Once you are happy with all of your settings, it's time to push that publish button. The first time will be a great feeling.

## Submitting to iTunes & Stitcher

Once we have our first episode published in our podcast hosting platform, we then can move to submitting our show to be included in iTunes & Stitcher. There are many other streaming services you can submit your show to, but iTunes & Stitcher will cover pretty much every mobile device there is. It won't hurt to be available in other places, but these are the only two I will cover.

### iTunes

To submit your new show to iTunes you will have to have an iTunes account. If you don't have one already you will be prompted to do so. Don't worry, it doesn't cost a thing.

Go to **PodcastingPro.com/itunes** for the submittal page.

The only thing you will need to do this is your RSS feed URL. In Libsyn you can find this in the Destinations tab.

Once you've entered your RSS feed it will pull in the information from Libsyn for you to review. If everything looks correct, click the submit button. It's that easy. You will get a confirmation email within the next hour letting you know that your show is under review. Within 1-14 days you will receive an approval or rejection email.

**Stitcher**

Submitting your show to Stitcher is a little more discretionary. You will first need to apply. Once approved, you will then need to also submit the same RSS feed you submitted to iTunes.

To apply, go to:
https://www.stitcher.com/content-providers

# Closing

It has been a great pleasure sharing the basics of getting started in podcasting. While a fun and rewarding activity, podcasting will no doubt come with its frustrations. There will be a time when you have technical difficulties and there will be times when the show content just didn't work. The important thing is to just keep doing.

The old saying "practice makes perfect" definitely runs true in the podcasting world. I started with probably the worst setup of all time four years ago and with more mistakes than I care to remember. Over 300 hours of published content later, I still feel like I learn something new every day. While this is a guide to get you set in the right direction, there is nothing wrong with experimenting with your own ideas or equipment. It's your show and your art.

When you feel comfortable and are producing content on a consistent basis, you will soon be able to leverage affiliate programs, get sponsors, and begin to make your show a profitable venture. One day, you may even get into the beast of live broadcasting your shows! Anything can happen and I hope to continue to help along the way.

Make sure to visit **PodcastingPro.com** for future podcasting books and to subscribe to my email list for tips and deals on podcasting products. We also offer personal consulting and editing services for those who find themselves in need of an all-in-one solution.

Thanks for your support and happy podcasting,

Orlando Rios

# Recommended Items

## Microphones
The Blue Yeti
GLS Audio ES-58
Shure SM7B

Find at **PodcastingPro.com/microphones**

## USB Mixing Boards
Mackie ProFX8v2 8-Channel Mixer
Behringer XENYX X1204USB Premium Mixer

Find at **PodcastingPro.com/boards**

## Software
Audacity
Adobe Audition
Garage Band

Find at **PodcastingPro.com/software**

## Hosting Services
Libsyn

Find at **PodcastingPro.com/hosting**

## Distribution Channels
iTunes
Stitcher

Find at **PodcastingPro.com/distribution**

Made in the USA
Columbia, SC
24 April 2018